AMAZING MAGIC™

GIMMICKS and CARD TRICKS

Illusions for the Intermediate Magician

Paul Zenon

rosen publishing's
rosen
central®

New York

North American edition first published in 2008 by:

The Rosen Publishing Group, Inc.
29 East 21st Street
New York, NY 10010

North American edition book design: Nelson Sá
North American edition editor: Nicholas Croce
Photography: Karl Adamson (tricks), Rich Hardcastle (remaining images)

Library of Congress Cataloging-in-Publication Data

Zenon, Paul.
Gimmicks and card tricks: illusions for the intermediate magician / Paul Zenon.
    p. cm.—(Amazing magic)
ISBN-13: 978-1-4042-1071-4
ISBN-10: 1-4042-1071-7
1. Magic tricks. 2. Card tricks.
I. Title.
GV1547.Z43 2008
793.8'5—dc22

                                                                2007008694

Manufactured in the United States of America

CONTENTS

Introduction • 4

Trick 1 • 5

Trick 2 • 14

Trick 3 • 21

Trick 4 • 30

Trick 5 • 36

Trick 6 • 40

Trick 7 • 46

Trick 8 • 51

Glossary • 57

For More Information • 59

For Further Reading • 61

Index • 62

INTRODUCTION

Magicians have more gadgets than James Bond—dozens of special devices known as "gimmicks" that enable them to work miracles. The reason you use a gimmick is to enable you to perform a trick that would otherwise be impossible or extremely difficult to do by sleight-of-hand alone. In this book I've selected several that have stood the test of time—you'll have seen them used by street magicians and mind readers in their TV shows.

Magicians also love card tricks—they usually make up the vast majority of their repertoires. The deck of cards is the ultimate magical device—fifty-two identities, thirteen values, four suits, and two colors allow for inexhaustible magical possibilities. When learning card routines, go for variety—you don't want every trick to consist of someone choosing a card and you finding it. The tricks in this book are not difficult—learn three or four that gradually grow in impossibility. And don't overuse them. Remember: always leave them wanting more!

TRICK 1

You pick up a saltshaker and pour the contents into your closed left fist. A snap of the fingers, and all the salt disappears. But it doesn't go far—it reappears pouring in a stream from your right hand!

The trick is made possible through a secret gimmick magicians call a "thumb tip." It's a hollow fake thumb, flesh-colored, usually made of plastic, and it fits over your real thumb. As you can see, they come in a variety of styles (1).

They're sold in magic and novelty stores the world over. Don't worry too much about the color matching your skin precisely; when it's used properly, it's not really in view of the audience and you'll use movement as added camouflage. It should fit loosely so that you can get it on and off your thumb easily, with room inside for whatever you're making disappear or appear. It's one of the most versatile gimmicks ever devised for the magician, and you'll find endless uses for it.

But first, let's learn how to use it to make a pile of salt disappear and then reappear. Start with the thumb tip in your right pocket. The saltshaker is on the table in front of you. As you pick the saltshaker up in your left hand, put your right hand in your pocket and get the thumb tip in place on your right thumb. Don't be self-conscious about the weird-looking blob of plastic: if you don't pay attention to it, no one else will. Let's imagine you're in a café, standing up with the saltshaker in your left hand (2). The photo shows your point of view.

You engage the spectators' attention with a bizarre story. "Have you ever seen people filling these saltshakers? Neither have I. You know why? They don't need to. The salt makes its way into the shaker all by

itself. I'll show you what I mean." With your right hand, take the salt-shaker from the left and, as you do, extend your right thumb so that it enters the left hand. Leave the thumb tip gripped and hidden in the left hand as you take the saltshaker away in the right (3).

Tip the saltshaker slightly and pour out a little of the salt, letting it fall to the table or floor. This is just to show that it's real. As you do that, the fingers of the left hand close into a fist and position the thumb tip so that it's open end upward, hidden in the hand. "I'll just use a little bit," you say as you openly pour the salt into the left hand and into the thumb tip (4), letting the salt flow out in a long thin stream from a good height above it. You don't actually pour very much salt into the thumb tip at all, but if you pour it right you can make it look like a lot.

Don't fill the thumb tip—a quarter- or half-full is enough: you have to leave enough room to get your thumb inside or the trick won't work. Put the saltshaker back on the table. As you do this, the fingers of your left hand work the open top end of the thumb tip back until it's projecting from the rear of the

fist (5). The fist tilts slightly toward the spectators.

No one should see you make this adjustment because the larger movement of putting the salt-shaker on the table covers the small movement of the left hand. "That might be a bit too much. Let me just get rid of those loose grains off the top." Your right hand now comes over the left as if to wipe off a few loose grains of salt. As it does, the right thumb is pushed into the thumb tip (6). The thumb tip is stolen away as your right palm makes a couple of brushing gestures across the top of your left fist. Move your right hand away with the back toward the audience and the thumb tip nearest to you so that it's behind your fingers (7).

Say, "Watch closely: we start with the salt in the left hand," and blow toward your left hand. Slowly open the left hand, finger by finger. "It's gone." Bring your palms together and brush both hands backward and forward a couple of times against each other as though the trick's over. The motion keeps the thumb tip invisible. Then drop both hands to your sides. "But it's not gone far. It's actually traveling up my left sleeve." Look toward your left sleeve as if following the salt as it

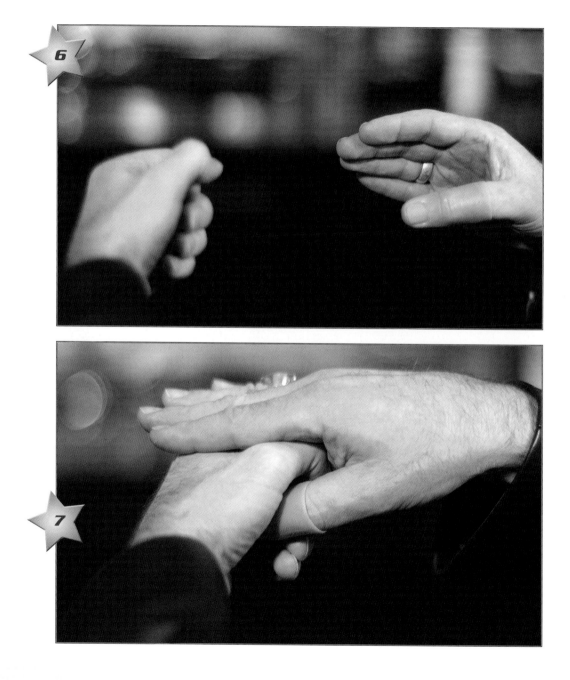

makes its journey. Shrug your left shoulder as if trying to shift the salt over a bony hurdle. "Oops. Over the shoulder. That's it—and across the back." Turn your head to the right as you continue to follow the imaginary migration. "Down the right sleeve— tricky little turn at the elbow. Along the wrist and . . . here it is!"

While you've been tracking the salt, you've closed your right hand into a fist with the thumb tip inside it and removed your thumb so that it's in much the same position in which it started in the left hand. Now raise your right fist and tip it over ever so slowly, allowing the salt to pour out in a fine stream (8). If you don't want to make a mess, catch it on a plate, in an ashtray, or in a cup.

When all the salt has poured out, reinsert your right thumb into the thumb tip and in a continuing motion brush your hands

together, the same as before, in what appears to be a natural move to wipe your hands clean of the last grains.

It also allows the spectators to see your hands apparently empty without inviting any close scrutiny.

NOTES

In this routine, the salt disappears from one hand and appears in the other, but you can make the salt appear from somewhere else entirely. One good way is to borrow a dollar bill. Show it on both sides and then roll it up into a tube around the thumb that has the tip on it. Leave the thumb tip with the salt inside the tube as you take it in the other hand. Wave your free hand over the tube in a pseudo-mystical way and then tip the tube over to pour out the salt. Stick your thumb back into the rolled bill and steal away the thumb tip as you unroll it and hand it back to the owner.

You can produce or vanish pretty much anything you can fit into the thumb tip. You can even use the gimmick to transform one object into another. For instance, to change salt into sugar you just need to have one or two sugar cubes palmed in your right hand. Perform the first part of the salt routine as written, secretly transferring the thumb tip into the left fist. Pour the salt into the fist and into the thumb tip.

However, as you steal the tip away on the right thumb you open the left fist a little and let the sugar cubes drop into it from the right hand. Tell the audience that you're going to transform the salt into sugar. "Now, you might be wondering how you'll be able to tell whether or not it's really changed; after all, they do look very similar. Well, it's easy: salt doesn't come in cubes!" You open your hands and tip the sugar cubes out onto the table.

A visit to your local magic shop or one of the many magic dealers on the Internet will reveal a whole variety of thumb tips for sale. These range from the cheapest, found in children's magic sets, to custom-molded prosthetic pieces created by special-effects technicians.

Whichever version you use, the real secret is to forget that you're wearing it. As mentioned earlier, it's not generally the color of a thumb tip that will give it away; it's more likely to be your body language while using it. One of the magic's greatest sleight-of-hand experts was Dai Vernon. Magicians called him "the Professor" because of his dedication and mastery of the craft. His greatest piece of advice to magicians was "Be natural." It's advice well worth following and can be applied to every single trick in this book.

TRICK 2

You're feeling lucky. You look at someone, write something on a pad of paper, and then ask the person to call out a number between one and ten. When you reveal your prediction, you're absolutely spot-on. You repeat the trick, this time asking two people to think of numbers. Again you write down your prediction. They call out their numbers and when they're totaled they add up to the very same number you wrote on the pad.

The secret gimmick used in this trick is called a "nail writer," sometimes known as a "swami gimmick." It comes in many different types, but basically they are all tiny bits of pen or pencil that can be attached to your thumb (1).

You use this gimmick to secretly write on the pad after the spectators have revealed the numbers they thought of. Writing with the nail writer isn't easy. You need to hold the pad with both hands. The right thumb should be at right angles to the surface of the pad (2).

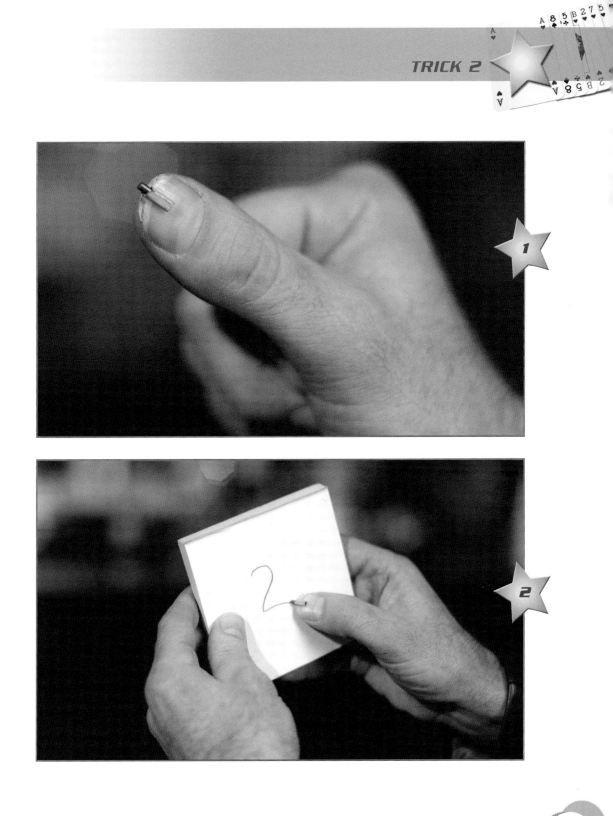

Learn to write in firm, bold strokes. And, having done that, learn to duplicate that style of writing when you use a pencil. It's no use if the writing made with the nail writer doesn't match the writing you would normally make with a pencil, especially in the routine that follows. Here's the presentation.

You have a pad, a pencil, and, assuming that you are right-handed, the nail writer on your right thumbnail. You don't have to worry about people catching a glimpse of the nail writer because it's so easy to hide it behind the pad you're holding. Start with a couple of psychological stunts to get the spectators in the right frame of mind. Write down the number seven on the pad, hidden from the spectators' view, and then ask everyone to quickly think of a number between one and ten.

Everyone can participate in this. Turn your pad around to reveal the number seven and ask how many people thought of this number. Sometimes an amazingly high proportion of your spectators will tell you that they did actually think of seven. This is simply psychology: seven is a number many people gravitate toward when asked to choose a number between one and ten. Tell the spectators this fact and comment on how much their choice reflected the findings of psychologists.

Sometimes it works and sometimes it doesn't. Tear off the top sheet of the pad and offer to try another experiment. "This time, think of a two-digit number between 1 and 50. It must be an odd number and the two digits should be different, so 22 doesn't count!" As they do, you write the number 37 on your pad. "OK: an odd number with two digits between 1 and 50. Did anyone get 37?" Turn the pad around to reveal the number. Again, a large percentage of your spectators will probably have thought of the same number. If you think about the options, the conditions you laid down really restrict which numbers they can choose and, of those, 37 is by far the most popular choice.

"Again, this isn't mind reading; it's psychology. If you analyze what I said, you'll see how I led you to the number 37. Let's try something else." Tear off the top sheet, and this time only pretend to write something down on your pad. Put the pencil aside or in your pocket. Select one of the spectators and ask him or her to listen very carefully. "I'm going to start calling out the numbers one to ten. At any time you feel like it, I want you to call 'Stop.' Stop me on any number you want, OK?"

Start calling out numbers. Make it interesting, calling them out fast and slow and with slightly different intonations as if working another psychological stunt and trying somehow to trap the spectator into choosing a particular number. If you get to the number ten before "Stop" has been called, start calling them out again backward. Sooner or later, however, the spectator should stop you on a number. Repeat that number and, as you do, hold the pad close to your chest and secretly write the chosen number on the top sheet with your nail writer while maintaining eye contact with the spectator. Asking the person why he or she stopped on that particular number will help give you time to do your secret writing, as well as provide misdirection for the action.

Finally, turn the pad around to show that you wrote down exactly that number. Tear off the top sheet, pick up the pencil, and tell the spectators that you'll try one final experiment. Pretend to write a two-digit number on the pad. Then place the pencil aside and hold the pad close to your chest. Select two spectators to help. Ask the first spectator to look at the second spectator: "Really study her."

"Look at the way she looks, the way she dresses, the color of her eyes. Now give me a two-digit number, quick as you can." The spectator follows your rather bizarre instructions and calls out a number. Let's say it's 27. Now ask the second spectator to return the

favor. She's to look at the first spectator and call out a number. Let's say she chooses 44. As soon as you know both numbers you mentally total them (27 + 44 = 71) and you secretly write this number on the pad. Then ask each of the spectators what they saw in the other that made them call out their numbers.

Make the most of their responses. "Well, unfortunately I didn't get 27 or 44," you say. Turn the pad around to reveal the number 71. "But here's the weird thing; you see, I wasn't just looking at one of you. I was looking at both of you." Pick up the pen and write the numbers 27 and 44 above your 71. Then openly add the two chosen numbers to reveal the total. The spectators will be amazed to see that they add up to 71—the same number you predicted. Ditch the nail writer in your pocket as you casually put the pencil away.

NOTES

It's difficult to write entire words with a nail writer, but it's not difficult to write down individual letters of the alphabet. You can therefore predict, say, someone's initials.

You can also easily mark ticks and crosses, so you could, for instance, write down a list of five animals and then ask someone to think of one. You appear to put a tick against one of the items on the list. In reality, you do nothing at all, but you nail-write a tick or cross against the thought-of animal as soon as the spectator has revealed it. You can do the same with a chosen number on a lottery ticket.

An impressive trick is to produce your prediction of a chosen number out of a sealed envelope. The envelope appears to make the use of any secret writing techniques an impossibility. In fact, it makes the use of a nail writer even more deceptive. Prepare for the trick by taking a blank business card or postcard and on it, in writing that matches your nail writer, write the phrase: "You will think of the number . . .," leaving the number part blank. The card is sealed in a small envelope, but unknown to the audience the envelope has a hole cut out of it and this hole lies immediately over the blank space.

To perform the trick, introduce the sealed envelope and place it on the table, hole side down. Ask someone to call out a number between one and ten. Pick the envelope up and open it. As you open it, use the nail writer to write the chosen number through the hole and on the card (3). Take the card out of the envelope and hand it to someone to read. While the person reads out the contents of the card, you ditch the envelope and nail writer in your pocket.

As I mentioned earlier, there are many different models of nail writer on the market. Some of them are modified thumb tips, others write with ink rather than pencil—although I've never found a reliable one of those. The best advice I can give you on the nail writer is "Practice, practice, and more practice." You need to be able to write without ever looking at your hands—and never write when other people are looking directly at your hands. The best time is when everyone's attention is elsewhere, usually on another spectator who is carrying out some task.

As with all magic, the secret is to believe you really can do what you claim. Then your body language doesn't give away the sneaky and sometimes complicated things you have to do to make the trick effective. And make sure you know the routine so well that the mechanics of it are working on an almost subconscious level: many a good trick has been ruined by a performer who hasn't rehearsed enough. Don't let that be you.

TRICK 3

You place a key in your hand, and it vanishes. You show a coin and squeeze it until it's bent in half. You take a handful of change from your pocket, and it disappears. These are just a few of the incredible effects made possible using a utility device that magicians call a "pull."

The most common type of pull works with a length of elastic. Thin black cord elastic is best. One end is tied to the object you want to make vanish—a key, for instance—and the other end is tied to a safety pin (1). The pin is fastened inside your jacket at the top of the right sleeve so that the key hangs down inside your sleeve, just above the edge of the cuff (2). In this position you can move the hand about freely and no one will spot the key.

When you want to perform the vanishing key trick, you casually bring the hands together and, with the left fingers, reach up the sleeve and pull the key down into the right hand. You don't want to be seen

1

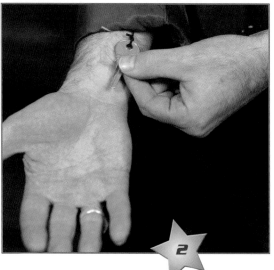

2

doing this preparation, so do it when the audience's attention is elsewhere. You can gain complete cover for the move by putting your hands behind your back while you do it. Either way, let's assume you now have the key secured in the closed fingers of the right hand.

Ask the audience if they've seen that guy on

television who pretends that he can bend keys using the power of his mind. And then tell them that you have been practicing. "It's not quite working out: let me show you what I mean." You reach into your pockets with both hands as if searching for a key. This is all bluff, because the key you're going to use is the one that's attached to the elastic pull.

Bring the right hand out of the pocket, holding the key at the fingertips (3). The point at which the key is tied is hidden by the right thumb and fingers. The elastic runs along the near side of the wrist and isn't visible to the audience. Hold the key up so that everyone gets a good look at it. Then breathe on it, explaining, "The first thing you have to do is

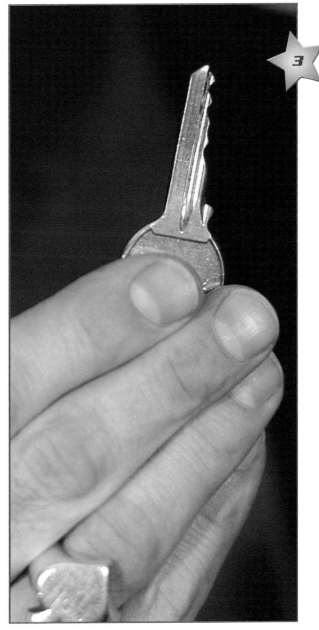

warm the key up slightly, like this." This is just an excuse to give them a decent chance to see the key in your hand. Open the left hand and place the key into it. The left fingers close around the key (4).

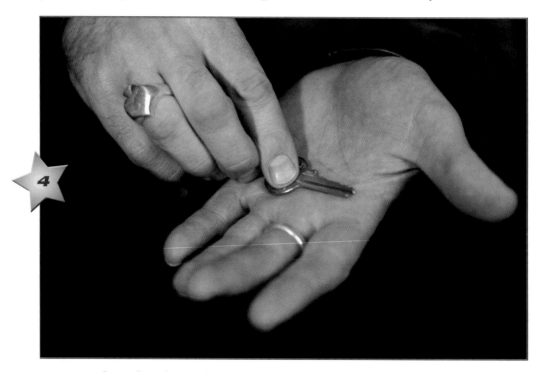

As they do, the right hand relaxes its grip on the key and allows the elastic to pull it quickly up the sleeve and out of sight. The right hand falls by the side as the closed left hand is held out for everyone to see. "Look—it's happening." Rub the fingers of the left fist together as if the key's becoming softer. Everyone will think that the key is somehow bending inside your hand. But you surprise them by slowly opening your fingers, one at a time, to reveal that the key has melted away completely. "It happens every time," you say. "I must be rubbing too hard!"

The Vanishing Key is just one of many tricks you can perform using a pull. Here are a few more variations.

Vanishing Coin

Instead of a key, drill a hole near the edge of a large coin. Attach one end of the elastic to the coin and the other end inside the sleeve as before. With this gimmick you can pretend to take out a coin from your pocket and make it disappear exactly as you did the key. It's a very clean disappearance and only requires a bit of acting ability to make it into a truly puzzling piece of magic.

Bending Coin

If you add a little sleight-of-hand, you can go even further. Get a coin that matches the coin you attached to the elastic. Cover it in a piece of cloth, and then bend it in half using a pair of strong pliers and a vice. The cloth prevents the coin from being marked by the tools while you're bending it. Have this bent coin in the right-hand jacket pocket and the coin on the pull in the right sleeve. This time, as you reach into the pocket to pull out a coin, you classic-palm the bent coin. Display the coin, which is attached to the pull at the fingertips and tell the audience about your amazing metal-bending powers. Pretend to place the coin in the left hand, but as you do, let the palmed coin fall into the left hand as the coin on the pull shoots up the right sleeve. Squeeze the coin in the left fist and ask someone to hold his or her hands out below, ready to catch the coin. "Be careful," you say. "It can get quite hot." Open the left fingers and allow the bent coin to fall into the spectator's waiting hands. The spectators won't just be surprised that the coin is now bent. If you "sell" the trick properly, many of them will be convinced that the coin is actually hot!

Disappearing Change

So far you've learned how to make disappear or change a single object, but using the pull you can make several objects disappear at once: at least, you could if you could prevent the objects rattling together as they traveled up your sleeve. Here's one simple way to meet that challenge. Using some superglue, make a gimmick that consists of several coins stuck together in a fan. The coins shouldn't all be the same denomination: you want to make the fan of coins look as if you could have picked it up from a handful of loose change.

The fan of coins has a hole drilled through it at one end and is attached to the elastic as before (5). This time, when you perform the trick you actually do take a handful of change from your left pocket.

5

Then you reach in among the change with the right hand, apparently picking up several of the coins. In fact, you don't pick any of these coins up. Instead, you push the fan of coins, which is already hidden in the fingers of the right hand, into view.

Hold the gimmicked coins up as if you've just taken them from the left hand (6). Drop the change back into the left pocket as you show the fan of coins. Pretend to place the coins in the left hand, but really allow them to shoot up the sleeve as usual. Close the left hand, wave the empty right hand over it and reveal that the coins have all disappeared. It seems absolutely impossible for a handful of coins to have completely evaporated under these conditions. Make the most of it. There's

one point to remember when making this gimmick. The elastic should be attached at the narrow end of the fan, not in the middle. This allows the gimmick to be drawn up the sleeve longways rather than sideways so that it doesn't catch on the edges of your sleeve.

NOTES

There's really no end to the variety of disappearances and transformations you can perform with a pull. The secret, as with most magic, is to be able to use the pull in a natural manner. You shouldn't look as if you're struggling to hold on to something that is attached to you. You have to behave as naturally while working the pull as if it didn't exist. As usual, any unnatural body language will make the audience suspicious.

Try different kinds of elastic until you get one that stretches easily, and adjust the position of the pull in your sleeve so that you can always get access to the object. It should lie a couple of inches above the edge of the sleeve when the elastic is relaxed, and the elastic should be strong enough that you can be confident it will quickly draw the object out of sight when necessary.

Equally important is the get-ready, the moment the left fingers reach up into the right sleeve to retrieve the pull. Always do this when no one's paying attention to you. If sitting, you can do it when your hands are below the table. If standing, take an opportunity to step back briefly from the action or behind someone or, as mentioned earlier, simply put your hands behind your back. Try to make the preparation a reasonable length of time before you go into the trick.

One final tip: some magicians prefer to have a pull that is elastic for most of its length but is actually fine fishing line for the last six

inches or so. They tie the length of elastic to the length of fishing line, and it's the fishing line that is attached to the coin or key. The reason for this is that the fishing line is virtually invisible and far less likely to be spotted by the audience than the much thicker black elastic. Try it: you might find it gives you far greater confidence and freedom when handling the gimmick.

TRICK 4

A spectator chooses a card from the deck, remembers it, and replaces it. The deck is cut several times and the card lost. But not for long, because you can find the card using a little forensic magic. One look at the spectator's thumb leads you to the only playing card in the deck that he's touched—the card he selected just moments ago.

This trick uses what's known as a key card. It's a card you spotted earlier in the trick and secretly positioned next to the selected card to help you to find it. Here's how it works. Take the deck of cards and hold it in your right hand in preparation for an overhand shuffle. Peel cards off the top of the deck into the left hand, just a few at a time, and ask the spectator to call out "stop" at any time (1).

When he does, stop taking cards, separate the hands, and thumb-off the top card of the left-hand packet. Ask him to take, look at, and remember this card. As he does this, your right hand tilts

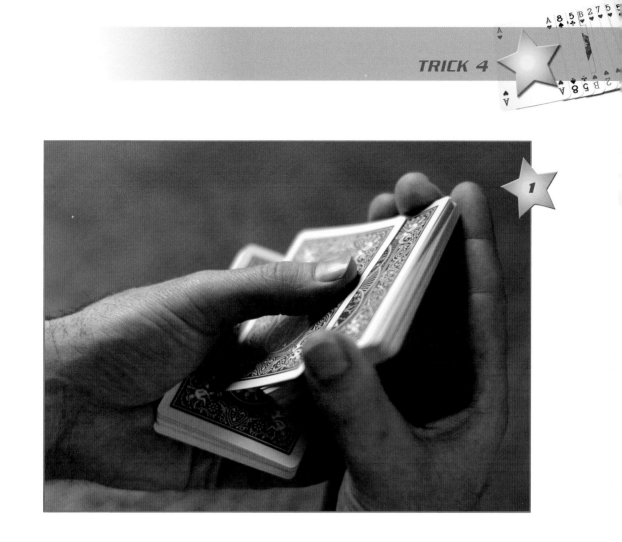

toward you so that you can take a sneak peek at the bottom card of the packet (2). This will be your key card. When the spectator has remembered his card, ask him to put it back where he got it from—on top of the left-hand packet. Immediately drop the right-hand packet on top of the left-hand cards. This puts your key card immediately above the spectator's selected card. Square the deck and give it a simple cut, cutting off the top half of the deck and placing it underneath the bottom half. "I'm going to give the deck two cuts and I want you to do the same." Make another cut and then hand the deck to the spectator. Ask him to do exactly what you did—give the pack two complete cuts.

Watch him to make sure he doesn't do anything other than that because, curiously, the cuts won't do anything to upset your trick but a shuffle would. When the deck is handed back to you, your key card will still be on top of the spectator's selected card. And because you've given the cards an even number of cuts, the chances are that they'll both be somewhere near the middle of the deck. Try it and see.

By this time the spectator should be convinced that you've no idea what or where his card is: you didn't see it, it went back into the middle of the deck, and the deck's been cut several times. How could you possibly find the card? Easy—forensic science! "Card tricks are a puzzle. They're like those crime stories you see on TV, a murder mystery. And you, my friend, are the murderer."

"Question is—who's the victim? I'm going to take a scientific approach. Can I see your thumb, please—your right thumb?" This request might get a puzzled look, but you insist on seeing his thumb. Persuade him to stick it up in the air as if hitching a ride, then pull it toward you and take a good look. If you want to get a laugh at this point, take out a magnifying glass and examine his thumb as if you were Sherlock Holmes.

"What I'm looking at is your thumbprint: everyone's thumbprint is different. And I noticed that when you chose your card you gripped it with your right thumb pretty much dead-center. You'll have left a big fat print there, my friend. Let me see if I can find it." Ask a different spectator to hold out his or her hand, palm upward, to play the part of a makeshift table. Start dealing cards from the top of the deck face-up onto his or her hand (3).

Tell the spectator who chose the card, "Now, I don't want you intimidating the witnesses by staring at them, so close your eyes for a moment." Continue dealing through the cards. Every now and then stop and pick up one of the cards from the face-up pile. Hold it alongside the spectator's thumb—the one who has his eyes closed—as if comparing the invisible print on the card with the print on his thumb. "Nope, that's not it: that's mine," you say, as you place the card back on the pile. Eventually you'll deal your key card on to the face-up pile. You now know that the next card dealt will be the spectator's. Stop as soon as you see it. "Get me a warrant. I think I've found it."

Take the card and hold it against the spectator's thumb for comparison. "Yep: that's the victim. Squeezed to death." Ask the

spectator to name the card he chose and then open his eyes. He should be amazed to see that it's the one you're holding.

NOTES

You don't have to spot your key card as the spectator takes his card. You can spot the bottom card of the deck before you even start the trick. That way no one will ever see you catch a glimpse of it. Often I'll make a mental note of the bottom card of the deck while the spectator is handling it during another trick. That way I can go straight into the trick and no one suspects a thing.

It doesn't matter how many times the deck is cut, the key card will always stay with the selection. The only exception is when the cards are cut so that the key card is the face/bottom card of the deck and therefore the last card you deal. If that happens, the chosen card will be the first card you dealt. That's no problem; just finish by pulling out the first card again from the bottom of the pile: the spectator who chose it has no idea where you plucked the card from—he still has his eyes shut!

TRICK 5

This is something your audience will always remember: a strange magical novelty in which you turn a spectator's credit card into a pretend Geiger counter. The credit card makes a clicking sound as it's dragged along the spread of cards on the table. As the clicking reaches its loudest point, you detect the chosen card!

As well as a spectator who's willing to lend someone as untrustworthy as you his or her credit card, you'll also need a marker pen with ink that will dry quickly when applied to a playing card. And for the yarn you're about to spin, the more unusual the pen looks, the better. Begin the trick by handing the pen out for examination, telling the spectator that it uses an ink that contains a specially formulated chemical. "Look—I'll prove it."

Ask if anyone has a credit card on them and then have that person select a card from the deck you're holding, but tell the person not to look at it. He or she is just to pull it from the deck and place it face-down on the table. "Great: now write your name on the back of the card." Hand the person the pen. As the person is writing on the back of his or her chosen card, you casually glance down at the deck in your hand and get a sneaky glimpse of the bottom card. This will be your key card. Put the deck on the table as soon as you've got the information. When the spectator has finished writing, take the pen back and put it away. "Now cut the deck in two." Point to what was the top half of the deck and ask the spectator to place his or her chosen card on it, and then to pick up the other half of the deck and place it on top of that. "Good. Now square the deck up and give it another cut. And another."

The spectator gives the deck two complete cuts. As mentioned previously, this cutting will not affect the position of your key card in relation to the spectator's card. They'll always be together apart from the 1-in-52 chance that they'll be the top and bottom cards of the deck. "Be honest: do you have any idea where your card is?" The spectator won't. "In fact, you not only don't know where the card is; you don't even know what it is, right?"

This is true. "That's where the special ink comes in." Pick up the deck and spread it across the table so that the index of all the cards can be seen. Ask the spectator to loan you a credit card. "This is going to sound a little odd. I told you that the ink in that pen was special. It is: in fact, it's . . . radioactive. And your credit card is a Geiger counter . . . don't look at me like that! I know it sounds a bit unlikely, but watch . . ." Take the spectator's credit card and slide its corner along the spread, from the face card to the top card (1).

Hold the card very lightly, pressing its corner onto the spread of cards. A faint clicking sound will be heard as the credit card trips off the edges of the playing cards. As you run the credit card along, look

out for your key card. The card directly next (underneath it in the face-up spread) will be the selection.

"I need to fine-tune this a bit . . ." Take the credit card and rub it on your sleeve as if trying to generate some static electricity or something. Then drag it along the spread of cards again, this time pressing down harder as the credit card nears the selection. As a result, the clicks get louder the nearer you get to the chosen card. Gently release the pressure on the credit card as you pass the chosen card. The clicks get softer again. Run the credit card along the spread a third time, this time creating the loudest clicks you can manage as you approach the selected card. "Got it!" Stop on the card and use the credit card to push it forward out of the spread. "There's only one way to know whether this is your card or not. Turn it over." The spectator turns over the card and finds his or her signature on the other side. Give back the credit card, saying, "I'd let that cool down for a while now if I were you!"

NOTES

The signature does mean that a card gets ruined every time you perform this trick, but I think it's worth it, and you can still use a deck that has half a dozen or more cards missing for many tricks without anyone noticing any difference in its thickness. The pen must, however, have quick-drying ink, otherwise it'll smudge and possibly mess up other cards. If no one trusts you enough to lend you their credit card (and if they had any sense, why would they?), you can use another distinctive playing card from the deck, for example, a joker or the ace of spades.

TRICK 6

You tell the spectator exactly what you're going to do to find his or her chosen card. Yet despite this and the impossible conditions under which the card is chosen, you make good on your promise, spelling out the phrase "This is your chosen card" to arrive at the selection. Best of all, the secret is so clever it might even fool you the first time you try it.

This trick introduces a new type of key card that you'll find useful in your magic. Instead of noting the face of the card, you put a slight bend in one of its corners, called a "crimp" (1). This means that you can locate it and cut to it again easily. An easy way to crimp the bottom card of the deck is to hold it in dealing position in your left hand and pull down on the inner right corner with your little finger (2).

If you're sitting at a table opposite your spectator, the crimp will be visible only to you, and you can put it in easily and secretly while

holding the deck and introducing the trick. "You might not know it, but there's a code among magicians—a set of rules that we stick to. For instance, we never reveal a secret. Well, not unless the money's right. And we never do card tricks on a Tuesday. Today's Tuesday? Well, I never was very good at sticking to the rules. But the most important rule of all is that we never reveal in advance what we're about to do. It just spoils the surprise and gives you a chance to catch me out, right? Well, I'm going to take a walk on the wild side and break that rule, too. I'm going to tell you exactly how this trick will end before it's even started."

By now you'll have crimped the corner of the bottom card of the deck and can start the trick proper. "Here's what I'm going to do: I'm going to ask you to take a card, remember it, and put it back in the deck, and then I'm going to use a magic spell to find it. In fact I'm going to spell the phrase 'This is your chosen card,' and I'll deal one card for each letter, like this . . ." You demonstrate by dealing cards from the deck onto the table, one card for each letter in the phrase "This is your chosen card." That's twenty cards in all.

Pick up the next card from the deck and turn it face-up as you say, "And the very next card will be yours. That would be amazing, wouldn't it? Well, I'd be amazed!" Put the card you've just shown back on top of the deck and then drop the deck on top of the pile of cards on the table. This positions your crimped card twenty-one cards up from the bottom of the deck. Square up the deck and leave it on the table.

"Let's start by choosing a card." Tell the spectator that you want him to divide the deck into three piles. Ask him to cut a really large packet of cards from the deck so that he just leaves a few cards on the

table. This large packet is placed to the right of the smaller packet. Now ask him to cut off a few cards from the large packet and place them to the right of that. This results in three packets of cards on the table with the largest in the middle, the former lower packet to its left and the former top packet to its right (3). The photo shows the spectator cutting off the last packet. You can see the crimped card in the middle packet.

3

"Now you've cut some cards from the bottom and you've cut some cards from the top: no one could know the name of the new top card." You point to the top card of the middle packet. It's absolutely true; no one could know the name of this card. Ask the spectator to take a look at it, remember it, and then put it back. "Let's lose your card so no one could possibly know where it is." Ask him to cut the large packet and complete the cut. He can give the packet several complete cuts until he's convinced that no one could know where his card lies. Take the packet from him, saying, "Of course, if I were a regular magician I'd be able to cut to your card like this." What you do is cut to the crimped card, taking it to the bottom of the packet. This is easy because the bent corner creates a break at the inner end of the packet. Hold the packet in your left hand when making the cut. The right hand comes over the cards, the fingers at the outer end of the packet and the thumb lifting up at the break at the inner end directly under the crimped card.

With practice you can make the cut without looking and send the crimped card to the bottom of the packet. "But that's not what I said I'd do: I said I'd spell to your card." Drop the large packet onto the small packet that originally came from the top of the deck—the one on the right. And then pick up the small packet from the left, which originally came from the bottom of the deck, and drop it on top of everything. The spectator won't notice that you didn't reassemble the deck in its original order. Bizarrely, everything is now set for you to spell out "This is your chosen card" and then turn up the next card to reveal the spectator's selection (4). It's true: because of the mathematics of the cutting and your crimp, the chosen card is now twenty-first from the top of the deck. Try it and see! You can add a line here that makes the trick even more convincing. "I said I'd spell 'This is your chosen card' and the next card would be yours. But it'd be even better if you did the spelling—here, take the deck." Hand the deck to the spectator and let him spell to his own card.

NOTES

Sometimes you get lucky when the spectator is cutting the large middle packet to lose his card; he might cut directly to the crimped card for you, saving you the task. From here on, it looks like a miracle where the trick has performed itself.

You can actually use any phrase you like in the spelling. It makes it more personal if you include the spectator's name: for example, "This is John's chosen card." The number of cards you spell out isn't critical, but around twenty is best.

TRICK 7

O ne of your spectators is also a cardsharp, but she doesn't know it yet. You ask her to cut the deck into four packets. She does. She then mixes the cards around a little and you ask her to turn over the top card of each packet. She does, and finds that somehow she's managed to find the four aces. How did she do it? She has no idea!

This trick is one of the easiest in the book and yet it's also one of the most impressive. Unknown to the spectator, you've already placed the four aces on top of the deck. Place the deck on the table in front of her and tell her, "I think you'd make a really good cardsharp: let me look at your hands." Take a good look at them and tell her how sensitive they look. "No, I'm serious! You've definitely got the makings of a cardsharp. Look; I'll show you what I mean."

Ask her to cut about a quarter of the cards from the top of the deck. She does. Then tell her to place this packet about a foot to the right of the rest of the deck (1). "Good. Let's do it again. This time,

cut about a third of the cards off." She cuts some more cards and you ask her to place them directly to the left of the previously cut packet. "Nice one; you are doing well." Bend down toward the table and squint at the cards as if gauging the number in each packet and trying to work out how many she should cut next. "This time, without thinking, just cut half the cards from the rest of the deck when I say 'Three.' Okay— one, two, three!" She makes the cut and places the packet to the left of the previous two packets.

This gives you four packets in a row. The four aces are now on top of the right-hand packet. "Have you ever done this before? No? You surprise me. Let's just even out the packets a little." Tell her to take the packet on the left and deal three cards from it onto the table at the spot from which she's just picked it up, then deal one card onto each of the other three packets (2). She then drops the packet back in its original position, but on top of the three cards she's dealt onto the

table. "I love the way you deal. Are you sure you never worked in a casino or anything?" Keep piling on the flattery and then ask her to pick up the next packet. Again she deals three cards down onto the table, into the same position the packet occupied, and then one card onto each of the other three packets.

She finishes by dropping the packet she is holding onto the three cards she dealt onto the table. "Great. I couldn't have done better myself. You really are good!" Ask her to pick up the third packet and repeat the procedure, the packet being dropped on top of the three dealt cards once again. Finally she picks up the right-hand packet. This is the packet that originally had the four aces on top. Because of the dealing, it now has three random cards on top of those aces. "Almost there: deal three cards onto the table and then deal one card onto . . . oh, you know the score by now."

She does the same again, and then drops the packet on top of the three cards she dealt onto the table. "Now, have you got any idea why you've been doing what you've been doing for the past minute?" She hasn't, so you explain: "You are a natural-born cardsharp. You cut the cards, and you mixed them up. But you also worked a bit of sleight-of-hand. How else can you explain this?" Slowly turn over the top card of each packet. Each one will be an ace (3).

NOTES

You can make this trick even more impressive by looking as though you give the deck a shuffle before you start. Start with the four aces on top. Secretly crimp the bottom card of the deck. Now pick up the cards in overhand shuffle position. Drop the top half of the deck or so into your left hand. The aces are now on top of this left-hand packet.

Drop the right-hand packet on top of the left-hand packet. This puts the crimp above the aces. Take the deck in your right hand again and shuffle a few cards off into your left hand. You can shuffle off as many cards as you like so long as you stop before you reach the middle of the deck: this is where the aces are located.

Now drop the rest of the right-hand cards on top of the left-hand cards. With the cards in your left hand, make a cut at the crimp so that the crimp is the bottom card of the upper packet. Complete the cut so that the crimp becomes the bottom card of the deck. This positions the four aces back on top ready for the trick. You can repeat this shuffle-and-cut sequence several times as you're talking. Done casually, it subtly suggests that the deck can't be set up—and so you're ready to blow them away.

TRICK 8

Holding the deck upright in your hand, you throw a cloth napkin, handkerchief, or headscarf over it. The cloth begins to move upward as a card rises from the deck. The card, still covered, floats about a foot into the air until it's caught by the performer. The cloth is whipped away to reveal that the card is—you'd better believe it—none other than one selected by the spectator!

This trick is unbelievably simple, but it looks really spooky. Have a card chosen, remembered, and replaced. Control it to the top of the deck: I do this using the crimp card method described earlier. Hold the deck in your left hand with the faces toward the spectators. Tell them that you'll use static electricity to accomplish this particular trick, so you'll need to insulate the deck. Funny how often that old static comes in handy for tricks, isn't it? Borrow a cloth napkin or headscarf and drape it over the deck (1).

Close your right hand into a fist and then extend your forefinger. Rub the forefinger backward and forward across your left sleeve as if

trying to generate some static—all just showmanship again, nothing to do with the actual method. Touch your forefinger to the top of the covered deck and then instantly pull your hand away as if you just felt an electric shock. Pause, rub the finger on your sleeve again, and

then touch it to the top of the covered deck once more. This time, with your left thumb you push upward on the top card of the deck. This is the one that was chosen. Keep pushing until the card pushes the fabric upward.

The spectators see something rising under the cloth. At the same time, raise your right hand so that it looks as if your finger is attracting the card and cloth and pulling them up with it (2).

Push the top card as far as it will go with your thumb and then extend your right little finger and hook it under the bottom edge of the card through the cloth (3). The photo shows an exposed

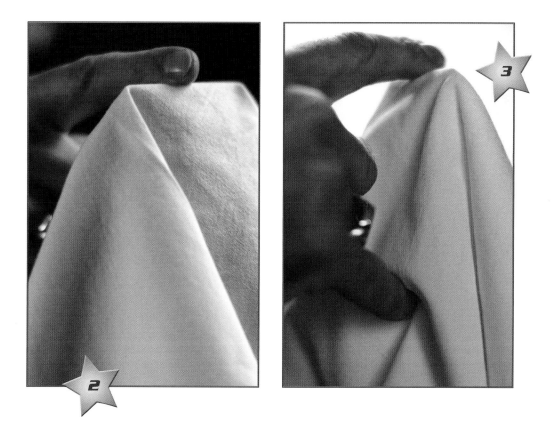

view, but so long as the spectators are standing in front of you they won't see this fiddle. You'll find that your right hand now has total control of the selected card. It's gripped between the forefinger at the top and the little finger at the bottom. Continue to raise your right hand high above the deck. From the front, it appears as if a card is floating in the air under the cloth: it looks really weird! (4)

Ask the spectator to name the card he chose. When it's about a foot or 18 inches (30 to 46 centimeters) above the deck, catch the top of the card between the right thumb and fore-finger and curl in your other fingers. Flip it upside-down so that the napkin falls over your hand to reveal the chosen card staring everyone in the face (5).

NOTES

This is a really cool trick. It is simple, yet it has a great effect on the audience. Obviously you can't have anyone standing next to you while you work it, otherwise that person will see how it's done, but other than that it's highly practical. The better your acting, the better this trick will be. Try to make it look as if that card really is floating under the handkerchief in the same way that a mime performer makes it look like a balloon is lifting him up into the air. Give it the practice it deserves.

GLOSSARY

classic-palm To hide a coin in one's palm, holding it without the aid of fingers.

crimp A bend made in the corner of a card so that it can be easily located visually or by touch and then controlled. The bent corner makes it easy to cut at the crimped card.

deck Another name for a pack of cards. Magicians usually use the term "deck" when talking about card tricks.

forensic The use of scientific knowledge to uncover legal mysteries. Loosely, the term "forensic" is used in magic to describe the processes used to make a trick successful.

Geiger counter An instrument used to detect the presence of radiation.

gimmick A hidden prop that the spectators don't know about. Magicians also talk about items being gimmicked. A fake coin, for example, could be described as a gimmicked coin.

gravitate To move toward or be attracted to something or someone.

key card A known card that indicates the position of a spectator's selected card. For instance you might know that the ace of spades is the bottom card of the deck. During the trick you position the ace of spades right next to the spectator's chosen card. You now know that whatever card is next to the ace of spades is the selection.

prosthetic A term that describes an artificial appendage.

pull A technique used by magicians to make objects appear to vanish. Used with a length of elastic, one end is tied to the object you want to make disappear with the other end tied to a safety pin. The pin is then attached to the inside of the sleeve.

repertoires A list or group of performances. In a magician's case, his repertoire is his library of different tricks.

sleight-of-hand Magic performed without the aid of devices, only the use of the performer's hands.

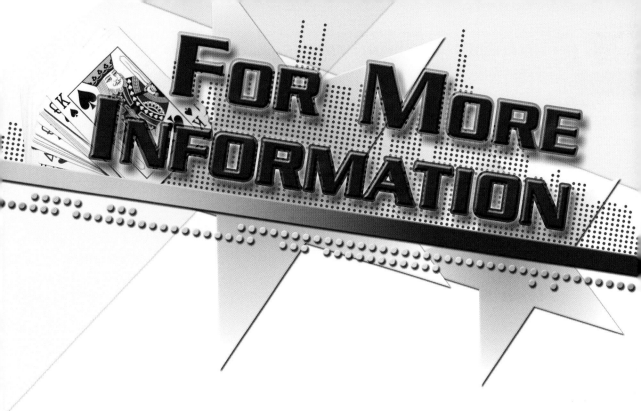

For More Information

Dr. Bob's Magic Shop
82867 Miles Avenue
Indio, CA 92201
(760) 342-3044
Web site: http://www.magicstor.com

Magic Hut
433 Lincoln Road
Miami Beach, FL 33139
(888) 42-MAGIC
Web site: http://www.magichut.net

Magic Max, Inc.
3728 Grissom Lane
Kissimmee, FL 34741
(407) 847-7552
Web site: http://www.magicmax.com

Magic Web Channel
P.O. Box 81391
Las Vegas, NV 89180
(702) 376-4727
Web site: http://www.magicwebchannel.com

Web Sites

Due to the changing nature of Internet links, Rosen Publishing has
developed an online list of Web sites related to the subject of this book.
This site is updated regularly. Please use this link to access the list:

http://www.rosenlinks.com/am/gctr

FOR FURTHER READING

Becker, Herbert L. *101 Greatest Magic Secrets Exposed.* New York, NY: Citadel, 2002.

Copperfield, David. *David Copperfield's Beyond Imagination.* New York, NY: HarperCollins Publishers, 1997.

Hugard, Jean. *The Royal Road to Card Magic.* Mineola, NY: Dover Publications, 1999.

Rourke, Dennis. *The Everything Card Tricks Book: Over 100 Amazing Tricks to Impress Your Friends and Family!* Avon, MA: Adams Media Corporation, 2005.

Scarne, John. *Scarne on Card Tricks.* Mineola, NY: Dover Publications, 2003.

Schiffman, Nathaniel. *Abracadabra! Secret Methods Magicians & Others Use to Deceive Their Audience.* Amherst, NY: Prometheus Books, 1997.

Severn, Bill. *Bill Severn's Complete Book of Magic: The Ultimate Book of Fascinating Illusions with Rope, Ribbon, String, Money, Coins & Mental Magic.* New York, NY: Galahad, 1998.

INDEX

A

ace of spades, 39

B

bluffing, 23
body language, 20, 28
Bond, James, 4

C

camouflage, 5
cardsharps, 46, 49
casinos, 48
change trick, disappearing, 26–28
children's magic sets, 13
classic palm, 25
close scrutiny, 12
coin trick, vanishing, 25
credit card trick, 36–39
crimp card method, 40–45, 49–51

D

denomination, 26
duplicating, 16
drilling holes, 25, 26

E

elastic pulls, 23–29
evaporation, 27

F

fine-tuning, 38
fishing line, 28–29
flattery, use of, 48
floating card trick, 51–56
forensic, 30, 32
four aces card trick, 46–50

G

gadgets, 4
gauging, 47

Geiger counters, 36, 37
get-ready, 28
gimmicks, explained, 4
gravitation, 16

H

handkerchiefs, 51, 56
Holmes, Sherlock, 33

I

imaginary migration, 11
intonations, 17

J

joker cards, 39

K

key card trick, 30–35
key card trick, crimped, 40–45
key trick, vanishing, 21–25

M

magicians' code, 42
magic/novelty stores, 5, 13
magic spells, 42
magnifying glass, 33
marker pens, ideal, 36, 39
mind reading, 4, 17
misdirection, 17

N

nail writer gimmick, 14–20

O

oft-chosen number, seven as an, 16
overhand shuffling, 30, 49

P

predicting, 14, 18
prosthetic pieces, 13
psychological stunts, 16, 17
pull devices, 21, 23–29

R

rehearsing, importance of, 20,
     44, 56

S

salt into sugar trick, changing, 12
salt trick, disappearing, 5–13
secret writing techniques, 18
sleight-of-hand, 4, 13, 25, 49
special-effects technicians, 13
static electricity, 51–52
street magicians, 4
superglue, 26
swami gimmick, 14–20

T

thumb tips, 5, 7–9, 11–13, 20
transformations, 28

V

Vernon, Dai, 13
versatility, 5

About the Author

Paul Zenon has dozens of TV credits to his name, including his own shows *Paul Zenon's Trick or Treat, Paul Zenon's Tricky Christmas,* and *White Magic with Paul Zenon.* He has also appeared on many other television shows, including *History of Magic, Secret History—Magic at War, The World's 50 Greatest Magic Tricks,* and many more. Zenon has performed in around thirty countries and in every conceivable location, from the Tropicana Hotel in Las Vegas to the hold of an aircraft carrier in the Adriatic; from the London Palladium to a clearing in the jungles of Belize; from the Magic Castle in Hollywood to the back of a truck in the Bosnian war zone.

Designers: Interior, Nelson Sá; Cover, Tahara Anderson
Editor: Nicholas Croce
Photography: Karl Adamson